I0471561

RIGHT TO INFORMATION ACT 2005

…in simple words

DEVENDRA KUMAR SINGH

M.Tech. (IIT Kanpur)
LL.B. (Campus Law Centre, University of Delhi)

ISBN: 9781638502302

Fifth Edition
October 2024

DEDICATION

This book is dedicated to all those unsung heroes who have strived hard to bring transparency and accountability in the working of Governments and their instrumentalities.

DEVENDRA KUMAR SINGH

ABOUT THE AUTHOR

Devendra, an M. Tech. graduate from IIT Kanpur, left his engineering career in year 2013 to raise awareness about RTI and other similar rights among needy persons. As an RTI practitioner since 2007, he has helped hundreds of such persons in exercising their rights without paying a single paisa in bribe. In last 5 years, he has helped dozens of victims of ATM/banking fraud in getting back their hard-earned monies using RTI Act.

Since 2015, Devendra has been imparting RTI trainings/lectures in Colleges/Universities/NGOs and Government departments to raise awareness about this Act. In year 2019, he delivered a lecture on RTI in a seminar jointly organized by Ministry of Human Resource Development (MHRD) and Central Information Commission (CIC) in New Delhi.

Devendra has completed RTI Internship in Ministry of Human Resource Development (MHRD) under DoPT's Annual Programme on "Improving Transparency and Accountability in Government through Effective Implementation of RTI Act". He has also interned with Association for Democratic Reforms - an NGO working in the field of Electoral Reforms and Transparency International India - an NGO working in the field of Anti-corruption.

Devendra has also studied LL.B. from Campus Law Centre, University of Delhi and is enrolled as an Advocate with Bar Council of Bihar.

He can be reached at rtidevendra@gmail.com.

PREFACE

More than 19 years have passed since the RTI Act was enacted. A large portion of our country's population is still unaware of this landmark tool. Out of those persons who know about this Act, there are many who have only read about it - in newspapers, in books or through social media - and have never submitted any request to obtain information under the Act. Out of those persons who have tried to get information by making request for it, many have stopped doing so because of no response or unsatisfactory response from the public authorities.

As an RTI practitioner for last 17 years, I have always felt the need of a guidebook which could help an applicant in drafting of RTI applications/appeals etc. The queries frequently raised by the audience, in the lectures delivered on RTI, have also led me to believe that a guidebook on this topic is required more than ever.

In government departments, there are many officers who have been designated as Public Information Officers to handle RTI requests, but they have not been given proper training on this subject. Because of this reason, they often fail to dispose of RTI requests in a manner provided by the Act. A guidebook is also required for these officers to help them understand the true meanings of the provisions of the Act on the basis of various judgments pronounced by the Courts on this subject.

Given the large-scale divide between the level of awareness of the RTI Act among citizens and the lack of training of Public Information Officers who deal with RTI requests in Government departments, it is time that a guidebook is published for the benefit of all. This book, in simple words, is an effort in that direction.

Devendra Kumar Singh

TABLE OF CONTENTS

INTRODUCTION

Before we proceed to understand what the Right to Information (RTI) is, let us recall the incidents where we had to pay bribe unwillingly to get our works done in government departments. In our country, which ranks 96th in Corruption Perception Index[1] ranking, it is not unusual to witness such incidents.

During field verification of your applications for Passport, Caste certificate, Income certificate, EWS certificate, PDS Ration card etc. or for availing the benefits of various Government schemes, you might have faced an ethical dilemma as whether to pay the *Kharcha- Paani* demanded by the Government officials or not. Your conscience would not have allowed you to pay the bribe, but the urgency to get your work done *in time* might have compelled you to give in. It is not the case that we do not want to fight corruption; the problem lies in that we do not know how to fight it.

---

[1] The corruption perception index ranks 180 countries by their perceived levels of public sector corruption.

Now, recall the incident when your application was stuck somewhere in a government department and you wanted to know the reasons for delay in your work. You might have also tried to meet authorities, but you were not given an opportunity for the same. You might have, then, felt the need to have known somebody who could make authorities listen to your grievances.

Be it the cases wherein Government officials demand bribe to do some work or the cases wherein the authorities do not listen to our grievances, the RTI Act is an effective tool to help us in these situations.

Right to Information

You might have read about Right to Information (RTI) in news or might have heard about it from your colleagues/family members/friends etc. If you are from Law background, there are chances that you might have studied RTI Act as a subject in your curriculum.

The term 'Right to Information', generally speaking, means citizens' right to get some information which the Government is holding. The question which naturally arises here is why a citizen needs information from the Government. This can be answered in the words of Justice A. P. Shah[2] as –
"Information is currency that every citizen requires to participate in the life and governance of the society. In any democratic polity, greater the access, greater will be the responsiveness; and greater the restrictions, greater the feeling of powerlessness and alienation. Information is basis for knowledge which provokes thought and without thinking process, there is no expression."

---

[2] Secretary General, Supreme Court of India v. Subhash Chandra Agarwal case, Delhi High Court 2010

The importance of 'knowledge' and the 'information' on which it is based, can be best understood in the words of *James Madison[3]*, an American philosopher –

"Knowledge will forever govern ignorance and the people who mean to be their own governors must arm themselves with the power the knowledge gives. A popular government without popular information, or the means of obtaining it, is but a prologue to farce or tragedy or perhaps both."

Freedom of Information

Freedom of Information (FOI) can be defined as the right to access information held by public bodies[4]. The terms Freedom of Information (FOI) and Right to Information (RTI) are used interchangeably. While FOI implies that the members of the public can access the information that the Government is holding, RTI reflects that public has a right to access the information.

Freedom of Information is an integral part of the fundamental right of freedom of expression, as recognized by Resolution 59 of the United Nations General Assembly adopted in 1946, as well as by Article 19 of the Universal Declaration of Human Rights (1948), which states that *the fundamental right of freedom of expression encompasses the freedom to "to seek, receive and impart information and ideas through any media and regardless of frontiers."[5]*

Freedom of Information Legislations in the World

Over the last several years, the right to information has been recognized by an increasing number of countries through the adoption of Freedom of Information (FOI) legislations. These

---

[3] Also, the fourth President of the United States of America

[4] http://www.unesco.org/new/en/communication-and-information/freedom-of-expression/freedom-of-information/

[5] https://www.un.org/ruleoflaw/thematic-areas/governance/freedom-of-information/

legislations reflect the fundamental premise that all information held by Governments and their instrumentalities are, in principle, public and may only be withheld if there are legitimate reasons, such as privacy and security, for not disclosing it.

Sweden was the first country in the world to adopt, in 1766, a law giving individuals the right to access information[6]. It took nearly two centuries before the next law was adopted in Finland in 1951. By 1995, only 19 countries around the world, mostly western democracies, had adopted RTI laws. In the last 25 years, the number of countries with such laws has grown from 19 in 1995 to more than 125 today.

Right to Information and Constitution of India

The Constitution of India does not explicitly grant a right to information. However, the Supreme Court of India has held in several cases that the right to information is implicit in the constitutionally enshrined rights to freedom of speech and expression (Article 19(1)(a)) and right to life and liberty (Article 21)[7].

In the case of **State of Uttar Pradesh v. Raj Narain[8]**, the importance of the people's right to know was described by **Justice Mathew** in the following words –
"In a government of responsibility like ours, where all the agents of the public must be responsible for their conduct, there can be but few secrets. The people of this country have a right to know every public act, everything, that is done in a public way, by their public functionaries. They are entitled to know the particulars of every public transaction in all its bearing. The right to know, which is derived from the concept of freedom of speech, though not absolute, is a factor which should make one wary, when secrecy is claimed for transactions which can, at any rate, have no repercussion on public security.

---

[6] "Recent spread of RTI Legislation" by World Bank Group
[7] www.humanrightsinitiative.org/programs/ai/rti/india/india.htm
[8] (1975) 4 SCC 428

To cover with veil of secrecy the common routine business, is not in the interest of the public. Such secrecy can seldom be legitimately desired. It is generally desired for the purpose of parties and politics or personal self-interest or bureaucratic routine. The responsibility of officials to explain and to justify their acts is the chief safeguard against oppression and corruption."

In the case of **S. P. Gupta v. Union of India**[9], Justice Bhagwati observed –

"No democratic government can survive without accountability and the basic postulate of accountability is that the people should have information about the functioning of the government. It is only if people know how government is functioning that they can fulfill the role which democracy assigns to them and make democracy a really effective participatory democracy. The citizens' right to know the facts, the true facts, about the administration of the country is thus one of the pillars of a democratic State.

It is now widely accepted that democracy does not consist merely in people exercising their franchise once in five years to choose their rulers and, once the vote is cast, then retiring in passivity and not taking any interest in the government. People should not only cast intelligent and rational votes but should also emeralds sound judgment on the conduct of the government and the merits of public policies, so that democracy does not remain merely a sporadic exercise in voting but becomes a continuous process of government - an attitude and habit of mind. But, this important role people can fulfill in a democracy only if it is an open government where there is full access to information in regard to the functioning of the government."

Right to Information legislation in India

In India, the first Supreme Court ruling on the right to information dates back to 1975. However, no attempt was made by either the Central or the State Governments to implement a simple and effective access to information regime until after the

---

[9] 1981 Supp (1) SCC 87

launching of campaigns for freedom of information by civil society.

The first and most well-known right to information movement in India was the **Mazdoor Kisan Shakti Sangathan (MKSS)**[10], which began its right to information work in Rajasthan during the early 1990s. MKSS's struggle for access to village accounts and transparency in administration is widely credited with having sparked off the right to information movement across India.

From the mid-1990s, a national campaign for the enactment of a central law on right to information gained momentum. After much struggle, the Central Government enacted the Freedom of Information Act in 2002. Unfortunately, a date for the Act coming into force was never notified and because of this reason, it never actually came into effect.

Right to Information Act, 2005

The Right to Information Bill was passed by the Parliament on 12th May 2005. President APJ Abdul Kalam gave his assent to the Act on 15 June 2005. The Act formally came into force on 12 October 2005.

During passage of the RTI Bill in Parliament, Prime Minister Dr. Manmohan Singh said[11] –

"I believe that the passage of this Bill will see the dawn of a new era in our processes of governance, an era of performance and efficiency, an era which will ensure that the benefits of growth flow to all sections of our people, an era which will eliminate the scourge of corruption, an era which will bring the common man's concern to the heart of all the processes of governance, an era which will truly fulfill the hopes of the founding fathers of our Republic."

---

[10] www.humanrightsinitiative.org/programs/ai/rti/india/india.htm
[11] https://cic.gov.in/valedictory-address-prime-minister

The preamble of the RTI Act, inter alia says that –

i.   It is "an Act to provide for setting out the practical regime of right to information for citizens to secure access to information under the control of public authorities, in order to promote transparency and accountability in the working of every public authority."

ii. It has been passed because "Democracy requires an informed citizenry and transparency of information which are vital to its functioning and also to contain corruption and to hold Government and their instrumentalities accountable to the governed."

THE RIGHT TO INFORMATION ACT

In order to make effective use of Right to Information (RTI) Act, it is imperative that we understand what this Act provides for. Only then, a person will be able to use this tool to contain corruption or to hold the Government accountable.

Understanding the use of RTI
Let us take an example.

Vinay, a daily wage labourer, wants to apply for a ration card. He has been asked to attach the photocopies of his Bank passbook and AADHAR Card along with the ration card application form. Vinay does not have any of these two requisite documents. He visits a bank in his locality to open a Savings bank account. The bank too asks for AADHAR card to open a bank account in his name.

Vinay, then, visits the nearest AADHAR enrolment centre to get enrolled. There, the AADHAR operator asks him to pay 100 rupees for the enrolment. As he knows from the UIDAI's advertisement that AADHAR enrolment is free of cost, he refuses to pay the money. The operator gets furious and does not enroll him. Vinay, then, dials the Unique Identification Authority of India (UIDAI) toll free number 1947 and lodges a complaint.

Around fifteen days have passed, and the AADHAR operator is still taking illegally money from the residents for the enrolment. Vinay wants to know from UIDAI what actions have been taken on his complaint. He tries to know it by again calling on the UIDAI toll free number, but is not satisfied with the response. He files an RTI application and requests the Public Information Officer of UIDAI to provide following information –

   i. How much is the fee for AADHAR enrolment
  ii. What actions have been taken by UIDAI on my complaint

Within 30 days of filing RTI application, he gets a phone call from UIDAI official who listens to his grievance and informs him about an enrolment centre where he can get enrolled free of cost. He also gets a RTI reply letter by post in which he is informed –

   i. AADHAR enrolment is free of cost.
  ii. On receipt of your complaint, UIDAI contacted 20 residents, who were enrolled at the same enrolment centre, to know whether they had to pay any fee for the enrolment. Based on their answers, the veracity of your complaint was established. The AADHAR operator has been blacklisted with immediate effect.

In the above example, Vinay was able to contain corruption and to hold the Government accountable with the help of RTI Act.

Salient Features of RTI Act, 2005

Before we proceed to learn how to make request for information under RTI Act, let us have a look at the various provisions of the Act. A prior understanding of the provisions of this Act will help us in drafting an effective application which will invariably result into a successful RTI case.

- Section 3 provides that all citizens shall have the right to information. This implies that persons other than the citizens of India cannot request for information under this Act.

- Section 5(1) provides that every public authority shall designate Public Information Officers to provide information to persons requesting for the information under this Act.

- Section 6(1) provides that any person, who desires to obtain any information under this Act, shall make a request to the Public Information Officer (PIO) of the concerned public authority.

- Section 7(1) provides that the PIO shall either provide the information within 30 days or reject the request for any of the reasons specified in sections 8 and 9.

  Where the information sought for concerns the life and liberty of a person, the same shall be provided within 48 hours of the receipt of the request.

- Section 7(2) provides that if the PIO fails to give decision on the request for information within the specified time period, the PIO shall be deemed to have refused the request.

- Section 19(1) provides that any person, who does not receive a decision within specified time period, or is aggrieved by a decision of the PIO, may prefer an appeal to First Appellate Authority (FAA) who is an officer, senior in rank to the PIO, in the same public authority.

- Section 19(3) provides that a second appeal shall lie with the Central Information Commission or the State Information Commission, as the case may be, against the decision of FAA.

- Section 20(1) provides that where the Information Commission is of the opinion that the PIO has, without any reasonable cause,

  - not furnished information within the specified period, or
  - malafidely denied the request for information, or
  - knowingly given incorrect, incomplete or misleading information, or
  - destroyed information which was the subject of the request, or
  - obstructed in any manner in furnishing the information,

  it shall impose a penalty of 250 rupees each day till information is furnished. However, the total amount of penalty shall not exceed 25,000 rupees.

Now, let us again look at the previous example, this time in the light of the provisions of the Act.

Vinay could request for information under RTI Act only because he was a citizen (Section 3).

He made the request for information to the Central Public Information Officer[12] (CPIO) of UIDAI (Section 6). UIDAI, the public authority, had designated Central Public Information Officers to provide information to persons requesting for the information under RTI Act (Section 5).

---

[12] The public authority UIDAI comes under the control of Central Government, hence the word Central Public Information Officer is used.

The CPIO provided the information within the specified period, i.e. 30 days (Section 7).

As Vinay was not aggrieved by the decision of the CPIO, he did not prefer any appeal to the First Appellate Authority, an officer senior in rank to the CPIO in the UIDAI (Section 19).

Had Vinay not received any reply from the CPIO within 30 days time or after having received the reply, had he been aggrieved by that decision, he could prefer an Appeal to First Appellate Authority (FAA) of UIDAI.

In case he was not satisfied with the decision of the FAA, he had the option to prefer an appeal to Central Information Commission (CIC).

Steps involved in an RTI case

The flowchart given below explains the steps involved in RTI cases–

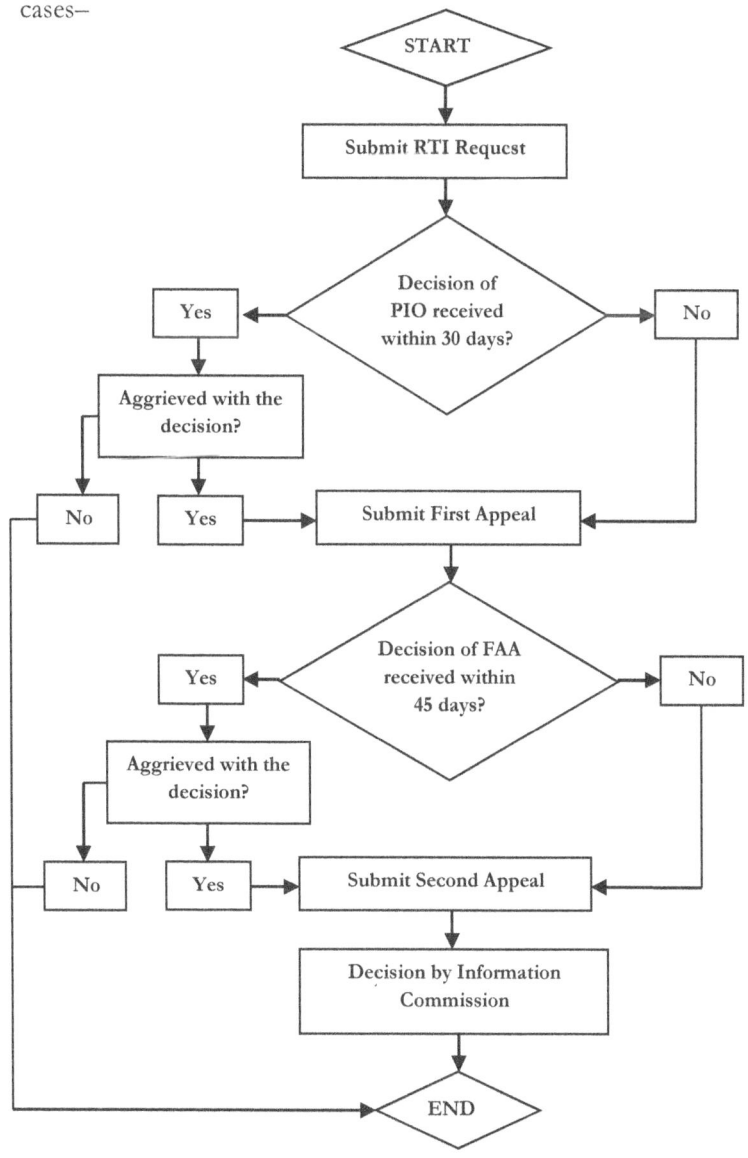

Every public authority designates Public Information Officer (PIO) to provide information to persons requesting for the information under this Act. An officer, which is senior in rank to the PIO, is designated as First Appellate Authority for deciding appeals preferred under the Act. The names and official addresses of these officers are generally made available on the website of the concerned public authority.

The definition of *"public authority"* has been provided under Section 2(h) of the Act. It means any authority or body or institution of self- government established or constituted –

- by or under the Constitution;
- by any other law made by Parliament;
- by any other law made by State Legislature;
- by notification issued or order made by the Government, and includes any –
  - body owned, controlled or substantially financed;
  - non-Government organization substantially financed, directly or indirectly by funds provided by the appropriate Government.

Certain organizations excluded from RTI Act

Section 24 of the Act provides that the Act shall not apply to the intelligence and security organizations specified in the Second Schedule. These are –

1. Intelligence Bureau
2. Research and Analysis Wing of the Cabinet Secretariat
3. Directorate of Revenue Intelligence
4. Central Economic Intelligence Bureau
5. Directorate of Enforcement
6. Narcotics Control Bureau
7. Aviation Research Centre
8. Special Frontier Force

9. Border Security Force

10. Central Reserve Police Force

11. Indo-Tibetan Border Police

12. Central Industrial Security Force

13. National Security Guards

14. Assam Rifles

15. Sashastra Seema Bal

16. Directorate General of Income-tax (Investigation)

17. National Technical Research Organization

18. Financial Intelligence Unit, India

19. Special Protection Group

20. Defence Research and Development Organization

21. Border Road Development Board

22. National Security Council Secretariat

However, the information pertaining to the allegations of corruption and human rights violations are not exempted from disclosure, even in these organizations.

THE RTI APPLICATION

Writing an RTI application is the most important step in an RTI case. The appeal provisions under the Act are only to ensure that information sought in the RTI application is provided to the applicant. Better understanding of the provisions of the Act will help us prepare a successful RTI case.

As whole of our discussion is about "information" and "right to information", it is imperative that, before proceeding further, we look at the following definitions given in the RTI Act –

- **Section 2(f): "information"** means any material in any form, including records, documents, memos, e-mails, opinions, advices, press releases, circulars, orders, logbooks, contracts, reports, papers, samples, models, data material held in any electronic form and information relating to any private body which can be accessed by public authority under any other law for the time being in force;

- **Section 2(j): "right to information"** means the right to information accessible under this Act which is held by or under the control of any public authority and includes the right to –

(i) inspection of work, documents, records;

(ii) taking notes, extracts or certified copies of documents or records;

(iii) taking certified samples of material;

(iv) obtaining information in the form of diskettes, floppies, tapes, video cassettes or in any other electronic mode or through printouts where such information is stored in a computer or in any other device.

Exemption from disclosure of information

It is equally important to know what kind of information cannot be disclosed under RTI Act. Section 8 of the RTI Act contains exemption from disclosure of information of certain kind.

Section 8(1) provides that there shall be no obligation to give –

(a) information, disclosure of which would prejudicially affect the sovereignty and integrity of India, the security, strategic, scientific or economic interests of the State, relation with foreign State or lead to incitement of an offence;

(b) information which has been expressly forbidden to be published by any court of law or tribunal;

(c) information, the disclosure of which would cause a breach of privilege of Parliament or the State Legislature;

(d) information including commercial confidence, trade secrets or intellectual property, the disclosure of which would harm the competitive position of a third party,

(e) information available to a person in his fiduciary relationship,

(f) information received in confidence from foreign Government;

(g) information, the disclosure of which would endanger the life or physical safety of any person or identify the source of information or assistance given in confidence for law enforcement or security purposes;

(h) information which would impede the process of investigation or apprehension or prosecution of offenders;

(i) cabinet papers including records of deliberations of the Council of Ministers, Secretaries and other officers;

(j) information which relates to personal information the disclosure of which has no relationship to any public activity or interest, or which would cause unwarranted invasion of the privacy of the individual

However, the information which cannot be denied to the Parliament or a State Legislature shall not be denied to any person.

Section 8(2) provides that in spite of the exemptions above a public authority may allow access to information, if public interest in disclosure outweighs the harm to the protected interests.

Section 10 provides that where a request for access to information is rejected on the ground that it is in relation to information which is exempt from disclosure, then, access may be provided to that part of the record which does not contain any information which is exempt from disclosure and which can reasonably be severed from any part that contains exempt information.

Request for obtaining information

A person, who desires to obtain any information, shall make a request to the Public Information Officer of the concerned public authority. Such request can be made in writing (offline

RTI application) or through electronic means (online RTI application, wherever possible). It can be made in English or Hindi or in the official language of the area in which the application is being made.

The RTI application shall –
   i.   specify the particulars of the information sought therein;
   ii. ordinarily not contain more than five hundred words;
   iii. be accompanied by a fee of 10 rupees.

The additional fee for providing information shall be charged at the following rates –
   i.   rupees two for each page in A-3 or smaller size paper;
   ii. rupees fifty per diskette or floppy;
   iii. for inspection of records – no fee for the first hour of inspection and a fee of rupees 5 for each subsequent hour.

No fee shall be charged from any person who is below poverty line. However, a copy of the certificate issued by the appropriate Government in this regard shall be submitted along with the RTI application.

An RTI applicant is not required to give any reason for requesting the information or any other personal details except those that may be necessary for contacting him.

Section 6(3) of the Act provides that where an application is made to a public authority requesting for information which is held by another public authority, the public authority to which such application is made, shall transfer the application to that other public authority within 5 days and inform the applicant immediately about such transfer.

Third party Information

Section 2(n) of the Act defines **"third party"** as a person other than the citizen making a request for information and includes a public authority.

Section 11 of the Act provides that where a PIO intends to disclose any information on a request made under this Act, which –

    i.   relates to or has been supplied by a third party, and

    ii.   has been treated as confidential by that third party,

the PIO shall, within 5 days, give a written notice to such third party and inform him that he intends to disclose the information, and invite the third party to make a submission regarding whether the information should be disclosed.

Where a notice is served by the PIO to a third party in respect of any information, the third party shall, within 10 days from the date of receipt of such notice, be given the opportunity to make representation against the proposed disclosure.

Such submission of the third party shall be kept in view while taking a decision about disclosure of information. The disclosure may be allowed if the public interest in disclosure outweighs in importance any possible harm or injury to the interests of such third party.

Making request for information

The steps involved in making a request for information are given in the following flowchart –

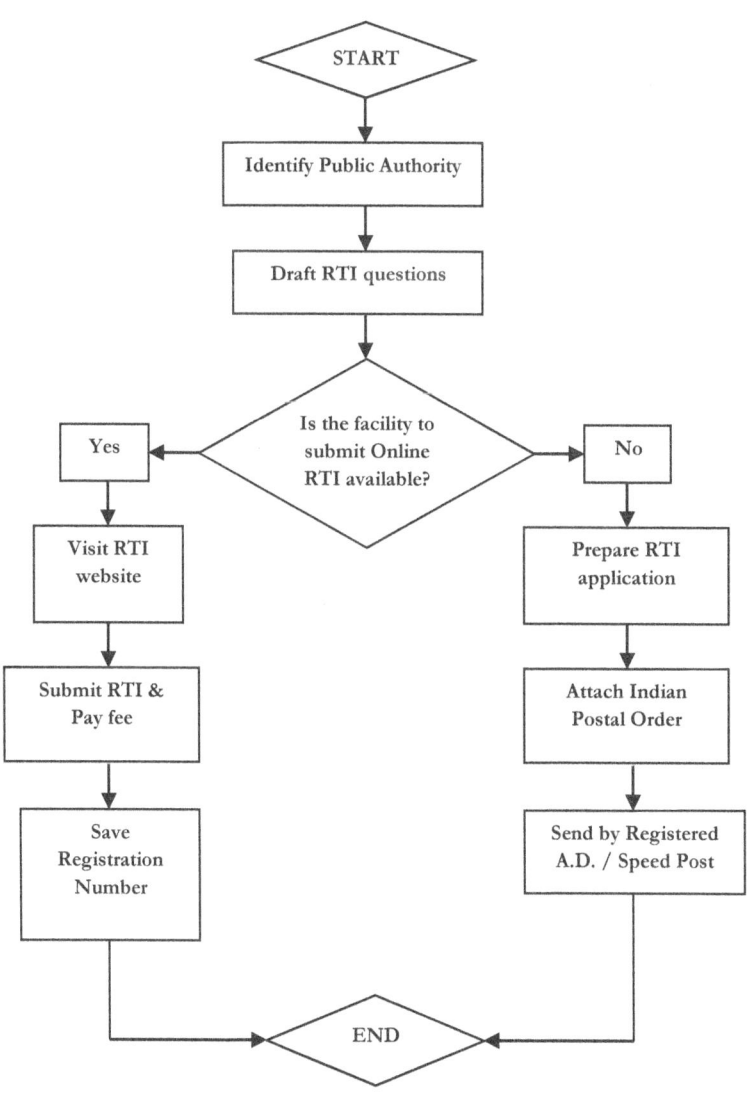

Online and Offline RTI Applications

A. Offline RTI application

A sample format of an offline RTI application is given below –

                                        Date –

To,

        The Public Information Officer,
        (Name of the public authority)
        (Office address of the public authority)

Subject – Request for information under RTI Act 2005

Dear Sir,

(Write background of the case, if required)

Particulars of Information sought

Please provide me information under following points –

1. (Write RTI question #1)
2. (Write RTI question #2)
3. (Write RTI question #3)
4. (Write RTI question #4)
5. (Write RTI question #5)
...

An Indian Postal Order worth Rs. 10 has been attached with this application as the fee specified under the Act.

                Thank you,

                        (Signature of the applicant)
                        (Name of the applicant)
                        (Address of the applicant)

In the AADHAR enrolment case, the offline RTI application could be written like this –

Date – 7th April, 2020

To,

The Central Public Information Officer,
Unique Identification Authority of India
Bangla Sahib Road, New Delhi-110001

Subject – Request for information under RTI Act 2005

Dear Sir,

Please refer to complaint number _____ dated _____ registered via UIDAI toll free number 1947 wherein it was reported that the AADHAR operator is illegally demanding money for enrolment process. Around fifteen days have passed, but I have not been informed of any action against the said operator.

Particulars of Information sought

Please provide me information under following points –

1. Please inform how much fee is prescribed for AADHAR enrolment.
2. Please inform me what actions have been taken so far by the UIDAI on my complaint.

An Indian Postal Order worth Rs. 10 has been attached with this application as the fee specified under the Act.

Thank you,

Signature.............
(Vinay Kumar)
H. No. 123, Kailash Nagar,
New Delhi, Pincode – 110001

B. Online RTI application

In those public authorities where online submission of RTI application is allowed, an applicant has the options of both online and offline submission. Online submission is cost-effective as it saves printing costs, postal charges etc. It is also preferred because the RTI applicant instantly gets the RTI registration number, using which he can check the status of his request anytime and submit the first appeal online, if required.

Online submission of RTI applications is allowed in almost all the public authorities under the control of Central Government. In a landmark judgment in March 2023, the Supreme Court had directed all the States / UTs and high courts to establish RTI web portals within three months to enable citizens to file RTI applications online. As of October 2024, 17 out of the 28 States have set up the facility of online submission of RTI applications and 11 states have not set up RTI websites.

The RTI web portals of Central Government and States of Uttar Pradesh, Maharashtra and Delhi are given below –

- Central Government - **https://rtionline.gov.in/**
- Uttar Pradesh - **https://rtionline.up.gov.in/**
- Delhi - **https://rtionline.delhi.gov.in/**
- Maharashtra -**https://rtionline.maharashtra.gov.in/**

Steps for Online RTI request

i.   Visit RTI web portal **https://rtionline.gov.in/**
ii. Click on **Submit Request** option.
     (Online RTI Request Form will be displayed.)
iii. Select **Ministry/Department/Apex Body** and **Public Authority** from dropdown boxes.
iv. Fill **Personal details of the RTI Applicant.**

v.   In the field **Text for RTI Request application,** write your RTI questions.

vi.   Click on **Make Payment** and pay Rs. 10 as fee.

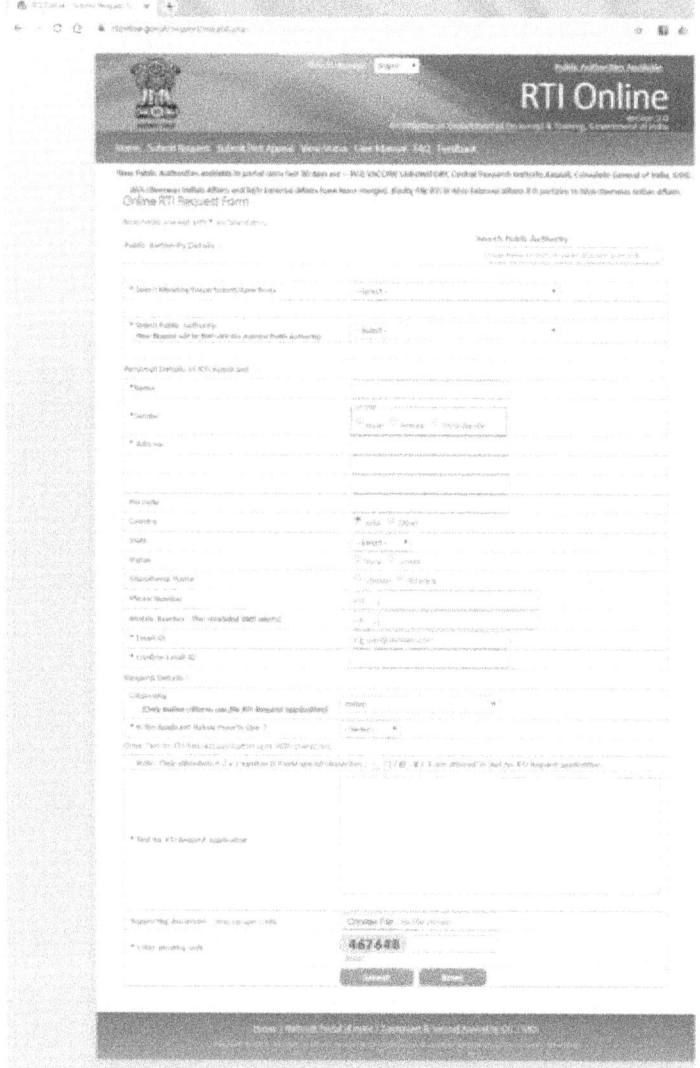

Upon successful payment of RTI fee, a **registration number** is issued. This number can be used, in future, for **viewing status** of your RTI application and for submitting appeal under the Act.

The steps shown above are for submitting RTI requests in Central Government offices. The procedure for submitting online requests on State RTI web portals is almost similar.

Drafting RTI questions

Drafting RTI questions is the most important part of any RTI request. This skill requires basic understanding of the various provisions of the Act. The success of the whole RTI case depends on this part itself. For example, if not carefully drafted, a request for information may straightaway get rejected in following cases –

i.   if the information sought does not fall under the definition of "information" given in Section 2(f)

ii.   if the information sought falls under the exemption specified in Section 8 and 9.

APPEALS UNDER THE ACT

After a request for information is submitted to the Public Information Officer (PIO), the ideal situation will be that the PIO supplies the information sought by the RTI applicant within the specified time period and the applicant is satisfied with the reply given. In this situation, no appeal is required to be submitted.

It may also happen that the RTI reply is not received, or if the RTI reply is received, the RTI applicant is not satisfied with the reply given to him.

An applicant, who does not receive any reply within the specified time period, or is aggrieved by the reply of the PIO, may prefer an appeal to the First Appellate Authority (FAA) within 30 days from the date on which the PIO's reply should have been received, or was actually received.

The FAA may admit the appeal after the expiry of the period of 30 days if he is satisfied that the appellant was prevented by sufficient cause from filing the appeal in time.

The appeal shall be disposed by the FAA within 30 days of the receipt of the appeal. The FAA may take upto a total of 45 days. However, the reason for delay has to be recorded in writing.

Let us have a look at the flowchart given below –

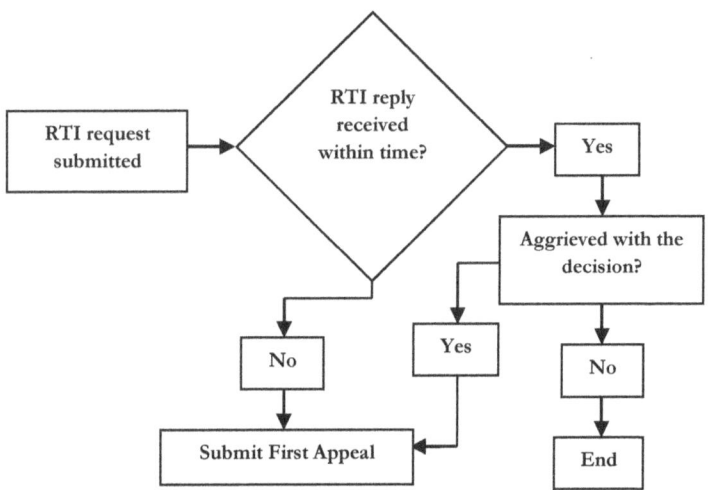

It is clear from the above flowchart that the first appeal needs to be filed in following two situations –

1) where RTI reply is not received
2) where the applicant is aggrieved with the reply

An appeal must always contain grounds for appeal and the prayers and relief sought.

Let us, now, learn how to write appeals.

First Appeal under RTI Act

A. Where RTI reply is not received

It is relatively easier to draft first appeal in this situation. The ground for appeal, here, is – "No response within the time limit." The prayers and relief sought may be the directions to the PIO for providing the information at the earliest.

An applicant needs to attach a photocopy of his RTI application, proof of payment of RTI fee and a photocopy of postal receipt, if it was sent by post, with the appeal.

A sample format of a First Appeal is given below –

Date –

To,

   The First appellate Authority,
   (Name of the public authority)
   (Office address of the public authority)

Subject – First Appeal under RTI Act 2005

Dear Sir,

I submitted a request for information under RTI Act to the Public Information Officer of (Name of the public authority) on (Date of making request). More than 30 days have passed since then, but there is no response from the Public Information Officer.

Therefore, I am submitting this appeal under the Act, with the prayer to give directions to the PIO to provide me the information at the earliest.

   Thank you,

     (Signature of the appellant)
     (Name of the appellant)
     (Address of the appellant)

Enclosures:
1. A copy of RTI application
2. A copy of Indian Postal Order attached with application
3. A copy of postal receipt

B. Where the applicant is aggrieved with the reply

The RTI applicant can also file an appeal with FAA when he receives a reply to his RTI application but is not satisfied with the reply given to him.

The reasons for dissatisfaction may be following –

I. If the PIO has refused access to the information requested

Section 7(8) of the RTI Act provides that where an RTI request is rejected by the Public Information Officer, he shall communicate to the applicant the reasons for such rejection.

The most common reasons given by PIOs for such rejections are –

   i. The information sought falls outside the definition of "information" given in Section 2(f) of the Act;

   ii. The information sought is exempted under any of the provisions of Section 8 or Section 9 of the Act.

   iii. The information sought is third party information under Section 2(n) of the Act; and the concerned third party has submitted representation against the said disclosure under Section 11 of the Act.

Section 7(2) of the Act provides that if the PIO fails to give decision on the request for information within the specified time period, the PIO shall be deemed to have refused the request.

II. If the PIO has provided Incomplete, Misleading or False information

Where the PIO has given a reply in time and has not cited any of the exemptions under the Act, but has provided Incomplete, Misleading or False information, the first appeal can be filed against his decision.

In all cases where an applicant is of the view that his request for information has been wrongly refused or he has not been given the information which he sought, he needs to mention the grounds of his appeal i.e. why he believes that he has been wrongly refused access to the information.

A sample format of First Appeal, in one such case, is given below –

Date –

To,

   The First appellate Authority,
   (Name of the public authority)
   (Office address of the public authority)

Subject – First Appeal under RTI Act 2005

Dear Sir,

I submitted a request for information under RTI Act to the Public Information Officer of (Name of the public authority) on (Date of making request). The PIO has refused access to information saying the information sought is personal in nature and has cited Section 8(1)(j) of the RTI Act.

I contend that the information sought in my RTI application is not the personal information, and even if it is so, public interest in disclosure outweighs the harm to the protected interests. Hence, it can be disclosed.

Therefore, I am submitting this appeal under the Act, with the prayer to give directions to the PIO to provide me the information at the earliest.

Thank you,

(Signature of the appellant)
(Name of the appellant)
(Address of the appellant)

Enclosures:

1. A copy of RTI application
2. A copy of PIO's reply

Second Appeal under RTI Act

A Second Appeal against the decision of FAA shall lie with the Information Commission within 90 days from the date on which the FAA's decision should have been made or was actually received.

The Information Commission may admit the appeal after the expiry of the period of 90 days if it is satisfied that the appellant was prevented by sufficient cause from filing the appeal in time.

Duty and Powers of Information Commission

It is the duty of the Information Commission to receive and inquire into a complaint from any person, who –

i.   has been unable to submit a request to the Public Information Officer either by reason that no PIO has been appointed or because the PIO has refused to accept his RTI application; or

ii. has not been given a response to a request for information within the specified time limit; or

iii. has been refused access to any information requested; and who believes that he has been given incomplete; misleading or false information.

The Information Commission has the powers to –

i. require the public authority to take any such steps as may be necessary to secure compliance with the provisions of this Act,

ii. require the public authority to compensate the complainant for any loss or other detriment suffered, and

iii. impose any of the penalties provided under this Act.

The decision of the Information Commission is binding.

Penalties under the Act

In any appeal proceedings, the onus to prove that the denial of a request was justified lies on the PIO, who denied the request.

1) Where the Information Commission is of the opinion that the PIO has, **without any reasonable cause**,

i. refused to receive an application for information, or

ii. not furnished information within the specified time period, or

iii. malafidely denied the request for information, or

iv. knowingly given incorrect, incomplete or misleading information, or

v. destroyed information which was the subject of the request, or

vi. obstructed in any manner in furnishing the information,

it shall impose a penalty of 250 rupees each day till application is received or information is furnished. However, the total amount of such penalty shall not exceed 25,000 rupees.

2) Where the Information Commission is of the opinion that the PIO has, **without any reasonable cause and persistently,**

i. failed to receive an application for information, or
ii. has not furnished information within the specified time, or
iii. malafidely denied the request for information, or
iv. knowingly given incorrect, incomplete or misleading information, or
v. destroyed information which was the subject of the request, or
vi. obstructed in any manner in furnishing the information,

it shall recommend for disciplinary action against the Public Information Officer under the service rules applicable to him.

The PIO shall be given a reasonable opportunity of being heard before any penalty is imposed on him. The burden of proving that he acted reasonably and diligently lies on the PIO.

Drafting Second Appeal

Drafting a second appeal is a little different from the drafting of first appeal. The major difference lies in the format of appeal and the prayers or relief sought therein.

As the Information Commission is empowered to order compensation to the appellant, impose penalty on the PIO, and recommend disciplinary action the PIO, the prayers and relief sought are accordingly modified.

Format of Second Appeal

Any person aggrieved by an order passed by the FAA or by non-disposal of his appeal by the FAA, may file an appeal to the Commission in the format given below –

1. Name and address of the appellant
2. Name and address of the PIO to whom the RTI application was addressed
3. Name and address of the PIO who gave reply to the RTI application
4. Name and address of the FAA who decided the First Appeal
5. Particulars of the RTI application
6. Particulars of the orders, if any, against which the appeal is preferred
7. Brief facts leading to the appeal
8. Prayer or relief sought
9. Grounds for the prayer or relief
10. Any other information relevant to the appeal
11. Verification/authentication by the appellant

The following documents are attached with the second appeal –
    i.   a copy of the application submitted to the PIO,
   ii.   a copy of the reply received, if any, from the PIO,
  iii.   a copy of the appeal made to the FAA,
  iv.   a copy of the order received, if any, from the FAA,
   v.   copies of other documents relied upon by the appellant, and
  vi.   an index of the documents referred to in the appeal.

A sample format of a Second Appeal is given below –

Date –

To,

The Central Information Commission
CIC Bhawan, Baba Gangnath Marg,
Munirka, New Delhi - 110067

Subject – Second Appeal under RTI Act, 2005

Dear Sir,

I submitted a request for information under RTI Act to the Central Public Information Officer of UIDAI on 07-Apr-2020. The CPIO refused access to information saying the information sought was personal in nature and exempted under Section 8(1)(j) of the RTI Act.

Against this order, I filed an appeal and contended that the information sought in my RTI application was not the personal information, and even if it was so, public interest in its disclosure outweighs the harm to the protected interests. Hence, it could be disclosed. The First Appellate Authority has re-affirmed the decision of the CPIO, but has not given any reason for it.

Therefore, I am submitting this appeal under the Act, with the prayer to give directions to the CPIO to provide me the information at the earliest.

Thank you,

Signature....
Vinay Kumar
H. No. 123, Kailash Nagar,
New Delhi, Pincode – 110001

Enclosures:
All the documents mentioned in the Index attached herewith

Online Submission of Second Appeal

Online submission facility of second appeal is available only in Central Information Commission (CIC). The second appeal can be filed in CIC only for the RTI cases belonging to public authorities under Central Government and Government of NCT of Delhi.

The procedure of filing appeal in CIC is given below –

i. Visit the website **https://dsscic.nic.in/online-appeal-application/onlineappealapplication**

A screen as shown in the following image will be displayed.

ii. Fill **Ministry/Department Details**
iii. Fill **Applicant's Particulars**
iv. Fill **Details of RTI Application**
v. Fill **CPIO Details**
vi. Fill **Response of CPIO**
vii. Fill **Details of First Appeal**
viii. Fill **FAA Details**
ix. Upload **Second Appeal application**
x. Upload **Supporting Documents**
xi. Upload **Applicant's ID Proof**
xii. Click on **Submit.**

On successful submission, the appellant gets a diary number by which he can view the status of his second appeal.

DEVENDRA KUMAR SINGH

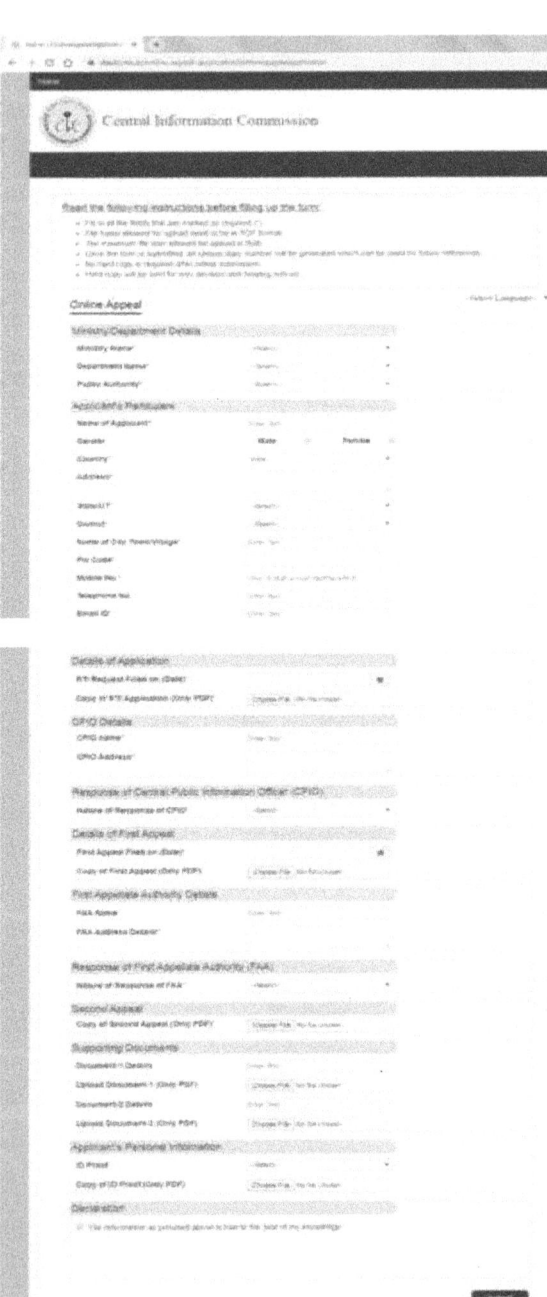

GRIEVANCE REDRESSAL THROUGH RTI

In many RTI cases, it has been observed that the applicants, in their requests for information, write more about their grievances and often do not specify exactly what information they are seeking from the PIO. In some cases, they ask for something which cannot be defined as information under Section 2(f) of the Act, and as a result, their requests get rejected.

We must always keep in mind that the RTI is "right to information", not the "right to investigation". We cannot simply submit RTI requests and expect our grievances to be redressed through it. RTI is not meant for registration of grievances.

There are several platforms, other than RTI, where a citizen's grievance can be registered and redressed. Some of these are –

    a.   President's Secretariat Helpline : **helpline.rb.nic.in**

    b.   Prime Minister Public Grievance Portal : **https://pmopg.gov.in/pmocitizen/Grievancepmo.aspx**

    c.   Central Public Grievance Portal : **pgportal.gov.in**

d. Uttar Pradesh Government's Public Grievance Portal : **http://jansunwai.up.nic.in**

e. Bihar Government's Public Grievance Portal : **http://lokshikayat.bihar.gov.in/onlinegrievance.aspx**

In almost every State, there is a public grievance portal available for the purpose of online registration and time-bound redressal of public grievances. If the online portal is not available, there is always an option to submit offline complaint in the respective department.

The appropriate way of seeking grievance redressal through RTI is-

i. First registering your grievance on public grievance portals, and thereafter

ii. Submitting an RTI request to know what actions have been taken on it.

In most of the cases, our grievances get redressed by registering it on Public Grievance portals itself. If any grievance is not redressed in a time-bound manner, we can submit an RTI request to know its status.

IMPORTANT JUDGMENTS ON RTI

Orders passed by Central Information Commission, or the State Information Commission, can be challenged in High Courts by the aggrieved party, by way of a writ petition under Article 226 of the Constitution. The Court judgments set out the correct interpretation of the provisions of RTI Act. In order to understand whether an information in a particular situation can be provided (or not) by the Public Information Officer, it is of utmost importance that the RTI applicants and the PIOs are aware of the Court rulings on the subject.

subject.

Let us have a look at the various judgments passed by the High Courts and the Supreme Court of India on various issues related to RTI Act –

A. Definition of information: Section 2(f)

Poorna Prajna Public School v. Central Information Commission: Delhi High Court [WP(C) No. 7265 of 2007]

"Information as defined in Section 2(f) of the RTI Act includes in its ambit, the information relating to any private body which can be accessed by public authority under any law for the time being in force. Therefore, if a public authority has a right and is entitled to access information from a private body, under any other law, it is "information" as defined in Section 2(f) of the RTI Act."

Khanapuram Gandaiah v. Administrative Officer: Supreme Court [SLP(C) No. 34868 of 2009]

"…an applicant under Section 6 of the RTI Act can get any information which is already in existence and accessible to the public authority under law. Of course, under the RTI Act an applicant is entitled to get copy of the opinions, advices, circulars, orders, etc. but he cannot ask for any information as to why such opinions, advices, circulars, orders, etc. have been passed, especially in matters pertaining to judicial decisions."

Central Board of Secondary Education v. Aditya Bandopadhyay: Supreme Court (Civil Appeal No. 6454 of 2011)

"The RTI Act provides access to all information that is available and existing. This is clear from a combined reading of Section 3 and the definitions of "information" and "right to information" under clauses 2(f) and (j) of the Act. If a public authority has any information in the form of data or analysed data, or abstracts, or statistics, an applicant may access such information, subject to the exemptions in Section 8 of the Act. But where the information sought is not a part of the record of a public authority, and where such information is not required to be maintained under any law or the rules or regulations of the public authority, the Act does not cast an obligation upon the public authority, to collect or collate such non-available information and then furnish it to an applicant."

Thalappalam Service Coop. Bank Ltd. v. State of Kerala: Supreme Court (Civil Appeal No. 9017 of 2013)

"Public authority, as already indicated, cannot access all the information from a private individual, but only those information which he is legally obliged to pass on to a public authority by law, and also only those information to which the public authority can have access in accordance with law."

Mannatil Kumar v. Central Information Commission: Kerala High Court [WP(C) No. 2261 of 2014]
"By making a request for obtaining information, an applicant under the Right to Information Act cannot expect a public authority to generate "information". The information already available on the records has to be supplied to the petitioner. Seeking redressal of grievance and obtaining information are different. As far as Right to Information Act is concerned, what is expected to be provided is regarding the information that exists in available files."

B. Definition of public authority: Section 2(h)

Indian Olympic Association v. Veeresh Malik: Delhi High Court [WP(C) No. 876 of 2007]
"…what amounts to "substantial" financing cannot be straight-jacketed into rigid formulae, of universal application. Of necessity, each case would have to be examined on its own facts. That the percentage of funding is not "majority" financing, or that the body is an impermanent one, are not material. Equally, that the institution or organization is not controlled, and is autonomous is irrelevant; indeed, the concept of non-government organization means that it is independent of any manner of government control in its establishment, or management. That the organization does not perform – or predominantly perform - "public" duties too, may not be material, as long as the object for funding is achieving a felt need of a section of the public, or to secure larger societal goals."

Northern Zone Railway Employees Cooperative Thrift and Credit Society v. Central Registrat, Co-operative Society: Delhi High Court [WP(C) No. 12210 of 2009]
"For an authority or body or institution to be classified as a public authority under clause (b) of Section 2(h), what is

necessary is that the authority, body or institution is established or constituted by a law made by Parliament. Parliament has not used the expression "under any other law made by Parliament". Therefore, the authority or body or institution should be created by, and come into existence by the statute framed by the Parliament, and not under the statute so framed."

Delhi Integrated Multi Model Transit System Ltd. v. Rakesh Aggarwal : Delhi High Court [WP(C) No. 2380 of 2010]

"Keeping in view the object of the Act, i.e. to bring about transparency in the working of all Government bodies and other public authorities – which are having Government control, i.e. they are not private entities, the expression "body owned ………by the appropriate Government" has to be given a wide meaning and interpretation. 50% ownership of the shares of a company of the appropriate Government, coupled with the strategic control that follows such shareholding, and which has been specifically incorporated in the Shareholder's Agreement and Articles of Association, is sufficient to clothe the petitioner with the character of a public authority under the Act."

"The process of decision making involves the choosing of one out of various available options. Where the appropriate Government is instrumental in the making of one choice over the other for a body/entity, it can be said that it has 'control' over the body/entity. 'Control' is that influence, which is attributable to the appropriate government by virtue of its role or position in the body. Such role should be ascribed to it, expressly or impliedly, either by law or by the constitution of the body itself, for example, in case of a company – by its Memorandum of Association, Articles of Association etc."

"…the meaning and scope of the term "Substantial", as occurring in the Act, has to be construed in contradistinction to the term "trivial" – that is to say it should not have small value/proportion/percentage so as to be insignificant. The meaning and scope of the term "finance" i.e. financial benefit could be in the form of share capital contribution or subsidy, or any other form including provisions for writing off bad debts, as also exemptions granted to the body from fee, duty, tax etc - for the purposes of Section 2(h) of the Act."

Indian Institute of Banking and Finance v. Mukul Srivastava: Delhi High Court [WP(C) No. 1856 of 2010]

"The mere subscription received by the Petitioner from its members, some of whom may be public authorities within the meaning of Section 2(h) of the RTI Act and the fees collected by it from the candidates who take the examinations conducted by it, cannot as such constitute 'substantial financing' by the 'appropriate government'."

Subhash Chandra Agrawal v. Office of the Attorney General of India: Delhi High Court [WP(C) No. 1041 of 2013]

"...the term "authority" as used in the opening sentence of Section 2(h) of the Act cannot be interpreted in a restrictive sense. The expression "authority" would also include all persons or bodies that have been conferred a power to perform the functions entrusted to them."

"...the expression "authority" as used in Section 2(h) of the Act would encompass any office that is conferred with any statutory or constitutional power."

Subhash Chandra Agrawal v. Indian Farmers Fertiliser Cooperative Ltd.: Delhi High Court [WP(C) No. 6751 of 2013]

"It is, no doubt, true that IFFCO is getting huge amount of subsidy from the Central Govt. but, in our opinion, it is not unique to IFFCO; subsidy is also being given to private sector players. The provisioning of subsidy is to keep the sale price of fertilizers low in open market so as to keep it within the reach of farmers. Subsidy is not a grant. It is only a mechanism to pay the difference between the cost of production and sale price of fertilizers. We, therefore, hold that subsidy cannot be construed as substantial financing of IFFCO."

Thalappalam Service Coop. Bank Ltd. v. State of Kerala: Supreme Court [Civil Appeal No. 9017 of 2013]

"Legislature, in its wisdom, while defining the expression "public authority" under Section 2(h), intended to embrace only those categories, which are specifically included, unless the context of the Act otherwise requires. Section 2(h) has used the expression "means" and "includes". When a word is defined to "mean" something, the definition is prima facie restrictive and where the word is defined to "include" some other thing, the definition is prima facie extensive. But, when both the expressions "means" and "includes" are used, the categories mentioned there would exhaust themselves. Section 2(h) exhausts the categories mentioned therein."

"We are of the opinion that when we test the meaning of the expression "controlled" which figures in between the words "body owned" and "substantially financed", the control by the appropriate Government must be a control of substantial nature. The mere "supervision" or "regulation" as such by a statute or otherwise of a body would not make that body a "public authority" within the meaning of Section 2(h)(d)(i) of the RTI Act."

"Merely providing subsidies, grants, exemptions, privileges etc. as such, cannot be said to be providing funding to a substantial extent, unless the record shows that the funding was so substantial to the body which practically runs by such funding and but for such funding, it would struggle to exist."

C. Definition of right to information: Section 2(j)

Poorna Prajna Public School v. Central Information Commission: Delhi High Court [WP(C) No. 7265 of 2007]

"The term "held by or under the control of any public authority" in Section 2(j) of the Act has to be read in a manner that it effectuates and is in harmony with the definition of the term "information" as defined in Section 2(f). The said expression used in Section 2(j) of the RTI Act should not be read in a manner that it negates or nullifies definition of the term "information" in Section 2(f) of the Act. It is well settled that an interpretation which renders another provision or part thereof redundant or superfluous should be avoided."

Registrar of Companies v. Dharmendra Kumar Garg: Delhi High Court [WP(C) No. 11271 of 2009]

"The definition of 'right to information' specifically qualifies the said right with the words: "accessible under this Act", and "which is held by or under the control of any public authority".

The information should, firstly, be accessible under this Act. This means that if there is information which is not accessible under this Act, there is no 'right to information' in respect thereof."

"A particular information may not be held by, or may not be under the control of the public authority concerned. There would be no right in a citizen to seek such information from that public authority, though he may have the right to seek the same information from another public authority who holds or under whose control the desired information resides."

D. Commercial confidence: Section 8(1)(d)

Naresh Trehan v. Rakesh Kumar Gupta: Delhi High Court [WP(C) No. 85 of 2010]

"In order to test the applicability of Section 8(1)(d) of the Act, it is necessary to first and foremost determine the nature of information and if the nature of information is confidential information relating to the affairs of a private entity that is not obliged to be placed in public domain, then it is necessary to consider whether its disclosure can possibly have an adverse effect on third parties."

The Institute of Chartered Accountants of India v. Shaunak H. Satya: Supreme Court [Civil Appeal No. 7571 of 2011]

"…the Appellant examining body is not liable to give to any citizen any information relating to question papers, solutions/ model answers and instructions relating to a particular examination before the date of such examination. But the position will be different once the examination is held. Disclosure of the question papers, model answers and instructions in regard to any particular examination, would not harm the competitive position of any third party once the examination is held."

"Therefore Section 8(1)(d) of the RTI Act does not bar or prohibit the disclosure of question papers, model answers (solutions to questions) and instructions if any given to the examiners and moderators after the examination and after the evaluation of answer scripts is completed, as at that stage they will not harm the competitive position of any third party."

General Manager Finance, Air India Ltd. v. Virender Singh: Delhi High Court (LPA No. 205 of 2012)

"Section 8 is an exemption to the otherwise regime of transparency and disclosure brought out by the Act. Naturally, the exemption cannot be allowed merely on the ground thereof being raised. It is for the public authority claiming exemption to lay foundation, of the information falling in one of the exempted categories."

Reserve Bank of India v. Kishanlal Mittal: Delhi High Court [WP(C) No. 1388 of 2012]

"...the Commission directed exclusion of the information which was exempt under Section 8(1)(d) of the Act, but that, in my view, was not a correct approach to deal with the matter. By doing so, the Commission left the whole thing to the discretion of the petitioner to decide as to which information would be exempt from disclosure and which information would not attract the exemption provisions contained in the Act. The correct approach, in my view, would have been to call upon the petitioner-bank to satisfy the Commission as to how and to what extent the information sought by the petitioner, included matters of commercial confidence, trade secret or intellectual property of the petitioner the disclosure of which would harm the competitive position of a third party and then, take a view in the matter. For this purpose, the Commission could also have examined such part of the information which the petitioner claimed to be exempt under Section 8(1)(d) of the Act, without disclosing the same to the respondent."

E. Fiduciary relationship: Section 8(1)(e)

Union of India v. R. S. Khan: Delhi High Court [WP(C) No. 9355 of 2009]

"...it will be no ground for the Union of India to deny to an employee, against whom the disciplinary proceedings are held, to withhold the information available in the Government files about such employee on the ground that such information has been given to it by some other government official who made the noting in a fiduciary relationship. This can be a ground only to deny disclosure to a third party who may be seeking information about the Petitioner in relation to the disciplinary proceedings held against her. The Union of India, can possibly argue that in view of the fiduciary relationship between the Petitioner and the Union of India it is not obligatory for the Union of India to disclose the information about her to a third party. This again is not a blanket immunity against disclosure. In terms of Section 8(1)(e) of RTI Act, the Union of India will have to demonstrate that there is no larger public interest which warrants disclosure of such information."

Indian Institute of Technology Delhi v. Navin Talwar: Delhi High Court [WP(C) No. 747 of 2011]

"...the evaluation of the ORS/ORM sheets is through a computerized process and no prejudice can be caused to the IIT by providing a candidate a photocopy of the concerned ORS. This is not information being sought by a third party but by the candidate himself or herself. The disclosure of such photocopy of the ORS will not compromise the identity of the evaluator, since the evaluation is done through a computerized process. There is no question of defence under Section 8(1)(e) of the RTI Act being invoked by the IIT to deny copy of such OMR sheets/ORS to the candidate."

Central Board of Secondary Education v. Aditya Bandopadhyay: Supreme Court (Civil Appeal No. 6454 of 2011)

"The term 'fiduciary relationship' is used to describe a situation or transaction where one person (beneficiary) places complete confidence in another person (fiduciary) in regard to his affairs, business or transaction. The term also refers to a person who holds a thing in trust for another (beneficiary). The fiduciary is expected to act in confidence and for the benefit and advantage of the beneficiary, and use good faith and fairness in dealing with the beneficiary or the things belonging to the beneficiary. If the beneficiary has entrusted anything to the fiduciary, to hold the thing in trust or to execute certain acts in regard to or with reference to the entrusted thing, the fiduciary has to act in confidence and expected not to disclose the thing or information to any third party. There are also certain relationships where both the parties have to act in a fiduciary capacity treating the other as the beneficiary. Examples of these are: a partner vis-a-vis another partner and an employer vis-a-vis employee. An employee who comes into possession of business or trade secrets or confidential information relating to the employer in the course of his employment, is expected to act as a fiduciary and cannot disclose it to others. Similarly, if on the request of the employer or official superior or the head of a department, an employee furnishes his personal details and information, to be retained in confidence, the employer, the official superior or departmental head is expected to hold such personal information in confidence as a fiduciary, to be made use of or disclosed only if the employee's conduct or acts are found to be prejudicial to the employer."

"…the words 'information available to a person in his fiduciary relationship' are used in Section 8(1)(e) of RTI Act in its normal and well recognized sense, that is to refer to persons who act in a fiduciary capacity, with reference to a specific beneficiary or beneficiaries who are to be expected to be protected or benefited by the actions of the fiduciary – a trustee with reference to the beneficiary of the trust, a guardian with reference to a minor/ physically infirm/ mentally challenged, a parent with reference to a child, a lawyer or a chartered accountant with reference to a client, a doctor or nurse with reference to a patient, an agent with reference to a principal, a partner with reference to another partner, a director of a company with reference to a shareholder, an executor with reference to a legatee, a receiver with reference to the parties to a lis, an employer with reference to the confidential information relating to the employee, and an employee with reference to business dealings/ transaction of the employer. We do not find that kind of fiduciary relationship between the examining body and the examinee, with reference to the evaluated answer-books, that come into the custody of the examining body."

"We may next consider whether an examining body would be entitled to claim exemption under Section 8(1)(e) of the RTI Act, even assuming that it is in a fiduciary relationship with the examinee. That section provides that notwithstanding anything contained in the Act, there shall be no obligation to give any citizen information available to a person in his fiduciary relationship. This would only mean that even if the relationship is fiduciary, the exemption would operate in regard to giving access to the information held in fiduciary relationship, to third parties. There is no question of the fiduciary withholding information relating to the beneficiary, from the beneficiary himself."

"Therefore, if a relationship of fiduciary and beneficiary is assumed between the examining body and the examinee with reference to the answer book, Section 8(1)(e) would operate as an exemption to prevent access to any third party and will not operate as a bar for the very person who wrote the answer book, seeking inspection or disclosure of it."

Union of India v. Col. V.K. Shad: Delhi High Court [WP(C) No. 499 of 2012]

"As a matter of fact, the person who generates the note or renders an opinion is presumed to be a person who is objective and not conflicted by virtue of his interest in the matter, on which, he is called upon to deliberate. If that position holds, then it can neither be argued nor can it be conceived that notes on file or opinions rendered in an institutional setup by one officer qua the working or conduct of another officer brings forth a fiduciary relationship. It is also not a relationship of the kind where both parties required the other to act in a fiduciary capacity by treating the other as a beneficiary."

THDC India Ltd. v. R. K. Ratauri: Delhi High Court [WP(C) No. 903 of 2013]

"...this Court is of the view that ACR grading/ratings as also the marks given to the candidates based on the said ACR grading/ratings and their interview marks contained in the DPC proceedings can be disclosed only to the concerned employee and not to any other employee as that would constitute third party information. This Court is also of the opinion that third party information can only be disclosed if a finding of a larger public interest being involved is given by CIC and further if third party procedure as prescribed under Sections 11(1) and 19(4) of the RTI Act is followed."

Union Public Service Commission v. G. S. Sandhu: Delhi High Court [WP(C) No. 4079 of 2013]

"The advice from UPSC is taken by the Disciplinary Authority, as a statutory requirement under the service rules applicable to an employee and wherever the Disciplinary Authority takes such an advice into consideration while recording its findings in the matter, the concerned employee is entitled to supply of such advice to him, as a matter of right. There is no relationship of master and agent or a client and advocate between the UPSC and the department which seeks its advice. The information which the department provides to UPSC for the purpose of obtaining its advice normally would be the information pertaining to the employee against whom disciplinary proceedings have been initiated. Ordinarily such information would already be available with the concerned employee having been supplied to him while seeking his explanation, along with the charge-sheet or during the course of the inquiry. The UPSC, while giving its advice, cannot take into consideration any material, which is not available or is not to be made available to the concerned employee. Therefore, the notings of the officials of UPSC would contain nothing, except the information which is already made available or is required to be made available to the concerned employee. Sometimes, such information can be a third party information, which qualifies to be personal information, within the meaning of clause (j), but such information can always be excluded, while responding to an application made to UPSC, under RTI Act. Therefore, when such information is sought by none other than the employee against whom disciplinary proceedings are sought to be initiated or are held, it would be difficult to accept the contention that there is a fiduciary relationship between UPSC and the department seeking its advice or that the information pertaining to such an employee is held by UPSC in trust. Such a plea, in my view, can be taken only when the information is sought by someone other than the employee to whom the information pertains."

Reserve Bank of India v. Jayantilal N. Mistry: Supreme Court (Transferred Case (Civil) No. 91 of 2015)
"Under Section 35A of the Banking Regulation Act, RBI has been given powers to issue any direction to the banks in public interest, in the interest of banking policy and to secure proper management of a banking company. It has several other far-reaching statutory powers."

"RBI is supposed to uphold public interest and not the interest of individual banks. RBI is clearly not in any fiduciary relationship with any bank. RBI has no legal duty to maximize the benefit of any public sector or private sector bank, and thus there is no relationship of 'trust' between them. RBI has a statutory duty to uphold the interest of the public at large, the depositors, the country's economy and the banking sector. Thus, RBI ought to act with transparency and not hide information that might embarrass individual banks. It is duty bound to comply with the provisions of the RTI Act and disclose the information sought by the respondents herein."

Satpal v. Central Information Commission: Delhi High Court [WP(C) No. 5057 of 2015]
"…personal information or details submitted by an employee to an employer for the purposes of his employment are expected to

be kept confidential. Plainly, the same cannot be available to all and sundry. However, if the competent authority is satisfied that a larger public interest warrants the disclosure of such information, the same can be disclosed, notwithstanding, that the same was available with the person in a fiduciary capacity."

"...it is also important to note that even though the information available to any person in a fiduciary capacity is exempt from disclosure in terms of Section 8(1)(e) of the Act; the said exemption is not absolute. If the competent authority is satisfied that a larger public interest warrants disclosure of such information, the same would have to be disclosed. The width of the exclusionary provision of Section 8(1)(e) of the Act does not extend to information, the disclosure of which is warranted in public interest."

F. Danger to life or physical safety: Section 8(1)(g)

Bihar Public Service Commission v. Saiyed Hussain Abbas Rizwi: Supreme Court [Civil Appeal No. 9052 of 2012]

"...let us examine the provisions of Section 8(1)(g) with greater emphasis on the expressions that are relevant to the present case. This section concerns with the cases where no obligation is cast upon the public authority to furnish information, the disclosure of which would endanger (a) the life (b) physical safety of any person. The legislature, in its wisdom, has used two distinct expressions. They cannot be read or construed as being synonymous. Every expression used by the Legislature must be given its intended meaning and, in fact, a purposeful interpretation. The expression 'life' has to be construed liberally. 'Physical safety' is a restricted term while life is a term of wide connotation. 'Life' includes reputation of an individual as well as the right to live with freedom. The expression ' life' also appears in Article 21 of the Constitution and has been provided a wide meaning so as to inter alia include within its ambit the right to live with dignity, right to shelter, right to basic needs and even the right to reputation. The expression life under section 8(1(g) the Act, thus, has to be understood in somewhat similar dimensions. The term 'endanger' or 'endangerment' means the act or an instance of putting someone or something in danger; exposure to peril or such situation which would hurt the concept of life as understood in its wider sense. Of course, physical safety would mean the likelihood of assault to physical existence of a person. If in the opinion of the concerned authority there is danger to life or possibility of danger to physical safety, the State Information Commission would be entitled to bring such case within the exemption of Section 8(1)(g) of the Act."

Union Public Service Commission v. G. S. Sandhu : Delhi High Court [WP(C) No. 4079 of 2013]

"As regards the applicability of clause (g), it would be seen that the said clause exempts information of two kinds from disclosure – the first being the information disclosure of which would endanger the life or physical safety of any person and second being the information which would identify the source of information or assistance given in confidence for law enforcement or security purposes. The two parts of the clause are independent of each other - meaning thereby that exemption from disclosure on account of danger to the life or physical safety of any person can be ground of exemption irrespective of who had given the information, who was the person, to whom the information was given, what was the purpose of giving information and what were the terms – expressed or implied subject to which the information was provided."

"…the person against whom an adverse advice is given may hold the employee of UPSC recording a note adverse to him on the file, responsible for an adverse advice given by UPSC against him and may, therefore, harass and sometime even harm such an employee/officer of UPSC, directly or indirectly. To this extent, the officers of UPSC need to be protected. However, the purpose can be fully achieved by blocking the name, designation or any other indication which would disclose or tend to disclose the identity of the author of the noting. Denying the notings altogether would not be justified when the intended objective can be fully achieved by adopting such safeguards."

G. Impede the process of investigation: Section 8(1)(h)

Bhagat Singh v. Chief Information Commissioner: Delhi High Court [WP(C) No. 3114 of 2007]

"Under Section 8, exemption from releasing information is granted if it would impede the process of investigation or the prosecution of the offenders. It is apparent that the mere existence of an investigation process cannot be a ground for refusal of the information; the authority withholding information must show satisfactory reasons as to why the release of such information would hamper the investigation process. Such reasons should be germane, and the opinion of the process being hampered should be reasonable and based on some material. Sans this consideration, Section 8(1)(h) and other such provisions would become the haven for dodging demands for information."

B S Mathur v. Public Information Officer: Delhi High Court [WP(C) No. 295 of 2011]

"The scheme of the RTI Act, its objects and reasons indicate that disclosure of information is the rule and non-disclosure the exception. A public authority which seeks to withhold information available with it has to show that the information sought is of the nature specified in Section 8 of RTI Act. As regards Section 8 (1) (h) of RTI Act, which is the only provision invoked by the Respondent to deny the Petitioner the information sought by him, it will have to be shown by the public authority that the information sought "would impede the process of investigation." The mere reproducing of the wording of the statute would not be sufficient when recourse is had to Section 8 (1) (h) of RTI Act. The burden is on the public authority to show in what manner the disclosure of such information would impede the investigation."

Deputy Commmissioner of Police v. Subhash Chandra Agarwal: Delhi High Court [WP(C) No. 8616 of 2011]

"...Section 8(1)(h) of the Act does not provide a blanket exemption in respect of all information that may be subject matter of any investigation. It only provides exemption from

disclosure of such information 'which would impede the process of investigation' or 'apprehension or prosecution of offenders'."
"Undisputedly, the information which is the subject matter of investigation can also be disclosed, provided that such disclosure does not impede such investigation."

Adesh Kumar v. Union of India: Delhi High Court [WP(C) No. 3543 of 2014]

"A plain reading of the aforesaid provision indicates that information which would impede the process of investigation or apprehension or prosecution of offenders could be denied. In order to deny information, the public authority must form an affirmative opinion that the disclosure of information would impede investigation, apprehension or prosecution of offenders; a mere perception or an assumption that disclosure of information may impede prosecution of offenders is not sufficient."

Central Board of Direct Taxes v. Satya Narain Shukla: Delhi High Court [WP(C) No. 5547 of 2017]

"…only such information which would (i) impede the process of investigation; (ii) impede the apprehension or prosecution of offenders, is exempted from disclosure by virtue of Section 8(1)(h) of the Act. In the present case, there is no material to indicate that any investigation is being conducted, which would be impeded by disclosure of the information sought for by the respondent."
"Even if, it is assumed that the verification being conducted by the Directorate General of Income Tax (Investigation) is in the nature of an investigation, the same is no ground for denial of information. Only such information which impedes the process of investigation can be denied. Thus, it would be necessary for the CPIO to specify the CIC that: (a) the investigation was conducted or was proposed; and (b) the information sought would impede the process of investigation. It is apparent that in the present case, these conditions are not met."

H. Disclosure of Cabinet papers: Section 8(1)(i)

Union of India v. Central Information Commission: Delhi High Court [WP(C) No. 8396 of 2009]

"The said sub-clause protects Cabinet papers including records of deliberations of the Council of Ministers, Secretaries and other officers. The first proviso however stipulates that the prohibition in respect of the decision of the Council of Ministers, the reasons thereof and the material on the basis of which decisions were taken shall be made public after the decision is taken and the matter is complete or over. Thus, a limited prohibition for a specified time is granted. Prohibition is not for an unlimited duration or infinite period but lasts till a decision is taken by the Council of Ministers and the matter is complete or over."

"The second proviso to Section 8(1)(i) of the RTI Act explains and clarifies the first proviso. As held above, the first proviso removes the ban on disclosure of the material on the basis of which decisions were taken by the Council of Ministers, after the decision has been taken and the matter is complete or over. The second proviso clarifies that even when the first proviso applies, information which is protected under Clauses (a) to (h) and (j) of Section 8(1) of the RTI Act, is not required to be furnished. The second proviso is added as a matter of abundant caution. Sub-clauses (a) to (j) of Section 8(1) of the RTI Act are independent and information can be denied under Clauses 8(1)(a) to (h) and (j), even when the first proviso is applicable."

Union of India v. Pramod Kumar Jain: Delhi High Court [WP(C) No. 14069 of 2009]

"It would be seen from a conjoint reading of the main Clause (i) and the first proviso to the said Clause, that though there is a prohibition against disclosure of Cabinet papers, which would include record of deliberations of the Council of Ministers, Secretaries and other officers, such prohibition as far as RTI Act is concerned, is not for all times to come and has a limited duration till the Council of Ministers takes a decision in a matter and the matter is complete or over in all respects. Considering the context in which the words "the matter is complete or over" have been used it appears to me that once the decision taken by the Council of Ministers has been given effect, by implementing the same, the prohibition contained in Clause (i) is lifted and the decision taken by the Council of Ministers, the reasons on which the decision is based as also the material on the basis of which, the said decision was taken can be accessed under the Right to Information Act."

I. Personal information: Section 8(1)(j)

Girish Ramchandra Deshpande v. Central Information Commissioner: Supreme Court [SLP(C) No. 27734 of 2012]
"The performance of an employee/officer in an organization is primarily a matter between the employee and the employer and normally those aspects are governed by the service rules which fall under the expression "personal information", the disclosure of which has no relationship to any public activity or public interest. On the other hand, the disclosure of which would cause unwarranted invasion of privacy of that individual. Of course, in a given case, if the Central Public Information Officer or the State Public Information Officer of the Appellate Authority is satisfied that the larger public interest justifies the disclosure of such information, appropriate orders could be passed but the petitioner cannot claim those details as a matter of right.

The details disclosed by a person in his income tax returns are "personal information" which stand exempted from disclosure under clause (j) of Section 8(1) of the RTI Act, unless involves a larger public interest and the Central Public Information Officer or the State Public Information Officer or the Appellate Authority is satisfied that the larger public interest justifies the disclosure of such information."

Bihar Public Service Commission v. Saiyed Hussain Abbas Rizwi: Supreme Court [Civil Appeal No. 9052 of 2012]
"Another very significant provision of the Act is 8(1)(j). In terms of this provision, information which relates to personal information, the disclosure of which has no relationship to any

public activity or interest or which would cause unwarranted invasion of the privacy of the individual would fall within the exempted category, unless the authority concerned is satisfied that larger public interest justifies the disclosure of such information. It is, therefore, to be understood clearly that it is a statutory exemption which must operate as a rule and only in exceptional cases would disclosure be permitted, that too, for reasons to be recorded demonstrating satisfaction to the test of larger public interest."

J. Severability: Section 10

Central Board of Secondary Education v. Aditya Bandopadhyay: Supreme Court (Civil Appeal No. 6454 of 2011)

"The answer book usually contains not only the signature and code number of the examiner, but also the signatures and code number of the scrutiniser/ coordinator/ head examiner. The information as to the names or particulars of the examiners/ co-ordinators/ scrutinisers/ head examiners are therefore exempted from disclosure under section 8(1)(g) of RTI Act, on the ground that if such information is disclosed, it may endanger their physical safety. Therefore, if the examinees are to be given access to evaluated answer books either by permitting inspection or by granting certified copies, such access will have to be given only to that part of the answer-book which does not contain any information or signature of the examiners/ coordinators/ scrutinisers/ head examiners, exempted from disclosure under section 8(1)(g) of RTI Act. Those portions of the answer-books which contain information regarding the examiners/co-ordinators/ scrutinisers/ head examiners or which may disclose their identity with reference to signature or initials, shall have to be removed, covered, or otherwise severed from the non-exempted part of the answer-books, under section 10 of RTI Act."

K. Third party information: Section 11

Poorna Prajna Public School v. Central Information Commission: Delhi High Court [WP(C) No. 7265 of 2007]

"…the term "third party" includes not only the public authority but also any private body or person other than the citizen making request for the information. The petitioner School, a private body, will be a third party under Section 2(n) of the RTI Act.

The above interpretation is in consonance with the provisions of Sections 11(1) and 19(4) of the RTI Act. Section 11 prescribes the procedure to be followed when a public information officer is required to disclose information which relates to or has been supplied by a third party and has been treated as confidential by the said third party. Section 19(4) stipulates that when an appeal is preferred before the CIC relating to information of a third party, reasonable opportunity of hearing will be granted to the third party before the appeal is decided."

"A private body or third party can take objections under Section 8 of the RTI Act before the public information officer or the CIC. In terms of Section 11(4) of the RTI Act, an order under Section 11(3) rejecting objections of the third party is appealable under Section 19 of the RTI Act before the CIC."

Arvind Kejriwal v. Central Public Information Officer, Cabinet Secretariat: Delhi High Court [WP(C) No. 6614 of 2008]

"…under the RTI Act, information that is totally exempt from disclosure has been listed out in Section 8. The concept of privacy is incorporated in Section 8(1)(j) of the RTI Act. This provision would be a defense available to a person about whom information is being sought. Such defence could be taken by a third party in a proceeding under Section 11(1) when upon being issued notice, such third party might want to resist disclosure on the grounds of privacy. This is a valuable right of a third party that encapsulates the principle of natural justice inasmuch as the statute mandates that there cannot be a disclosure of information pertaining to or which "relates to" such third party without affording such third party an opportunity of being heard on whether such disclosure should be ordered. This is a procedural safeguard that has been inserted in the RTI Act to balance the rights of privacy and the public interest involved in disclosure of such information. Whether one should trump the other is ultimately for the information officer to decide in the facts of a given case."

Union of India v. R Jayachandran: Delhi High Court [WP(C) No. 3406 of 2012]

"…this Court is of the view that the proper approach to be adopted in cases where personal information with regard to third parties is asked is first to determine whether information sought falls under Section 8(1)(j) of the RTI Act and if the Court/Tribunal reaches the conclusion that aforesaid exemption is not attracted, then the third party procedure referred to in Section 11(1) of the RTI Act must be followed before releasing the information."

L. Act to have overriding effect: Section 22

Poorna Prajna Public School v. Central Information Commission: Delhi High Court [WP(C) No. 7265 of 2007]

"Section 22 of the RTI Act is an overriding clause but it does not modify any other statute or enactment, on the question of right and power of a public authority to call for information relating to a private body. A bar, prohibition or restriction in a statutory enactment, before information can be accessed by a public authority, continues to apply and is not obliterated by section 22 of the RTI Act. Section 2(f) of the RTI Act does not bring about any modification or amendment in any other enactment, which bars or prohibits or imposes pre-condition for accessing information from private bodies. Rather, it upholds and accepts the said position when it uses the expression "which can be accessed" i.e. the public authority should be in a position and entitled to ask for the said information. Section 22 of the RTI Act, an overriding provision does not mitigate against the said interpretation for there is no contradiction or conflict between the provisions of Section 2(f) of the RTI Act and other statutory enactments/law. Section 22 will apply only when there is a conflict between the RTI Act and Official Secrets Act or any other enactment."

CONCLUSION

Our discussion on this subject ends here. We have gained much knowledge about RTI Act and the procedures to be followed while requesting for information therein.

Thomas Fuller, An English clergymen and author, once said, **"Knowledge is a treasure, but Practice is the Key to it."**

The author expects from his readers that, to get their works done in Government departments, they will submit RTI applications instead of offering bribe money. Only by doing this exercise repeatedly, they will be able to gain practical knowledge in this field.

Feedback
For an author, nothing is more valuable than the honest feedback provided by the readers of his book. If you have enjoyed reading this book, please write a review on Amazon or Flipkart, or whichever website you bought this book from.